Christmas
Activity Book for Toddlers

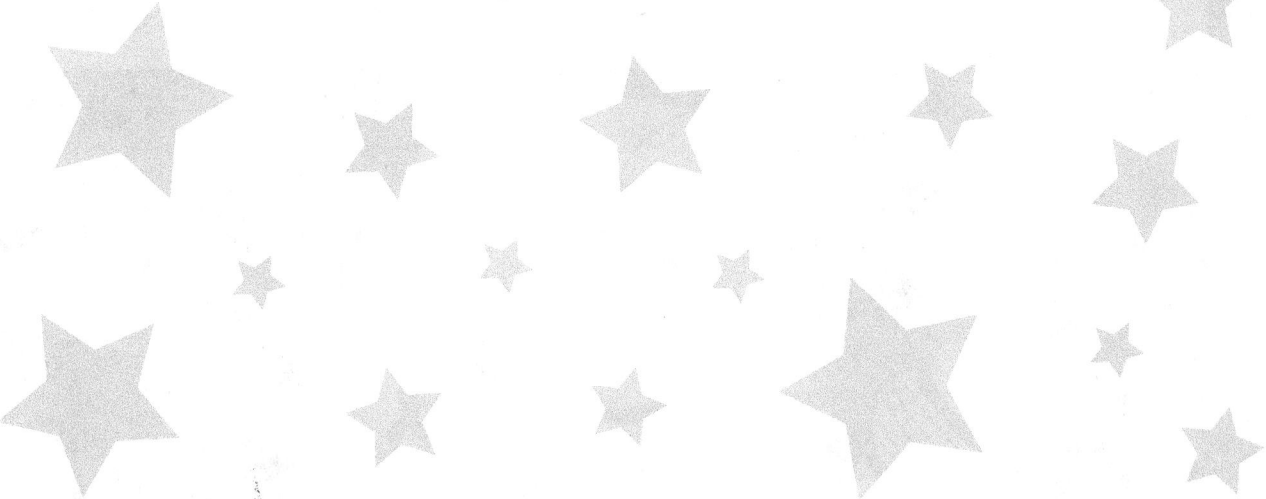

This book belongs to

I see .... Santa

one

I see ......2...... sleighs

two

2 2 2

I see ....3.... trees

three

3 3 3

I see ....4...... gingerbreads

four

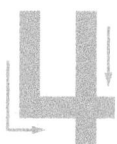 4   4

I see ....5.... gifts

five

5 5 5

I see 6 ornaments

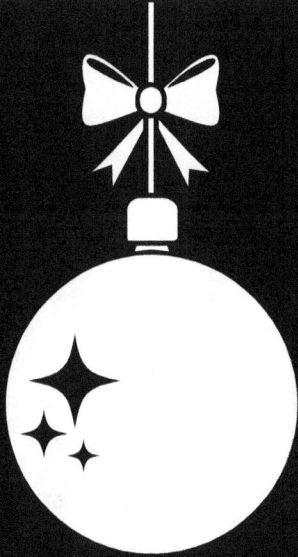

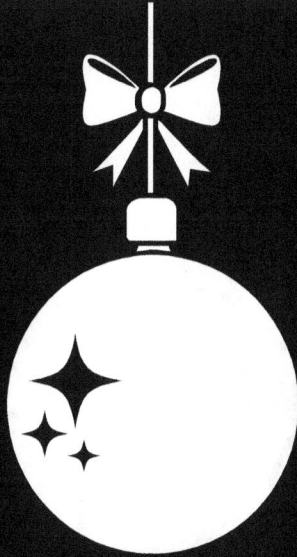

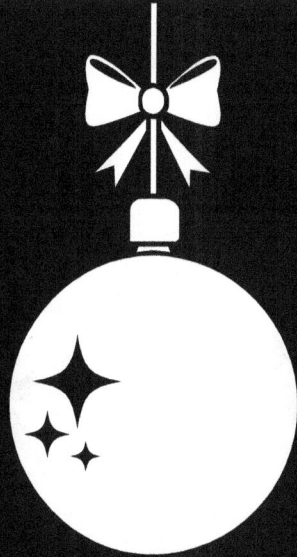

six

6 6 6

I see ....7.... candy canes

seven

7 7 7

I see ⁸ reindeer

eight

8 8 8

I see ....9.... desserts

nine

9   9   9

I see .... 10 bells

ten

10   10   10

I see .... || .... owls

eleven

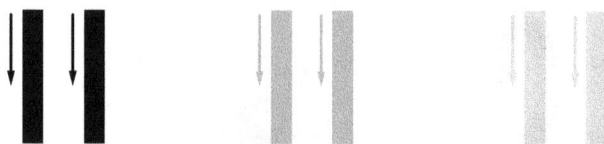

I see 12 snow globes

twelve

I see 13 mistletoes

thirteen

13 13 13

I see ....14.... coats

fourteen

 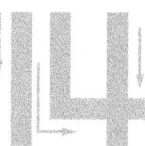 

I see ....15.... candles

fifteen

15 15 15

I see .... 16 bears

sixteen

16 16 16

I see 17 stockings

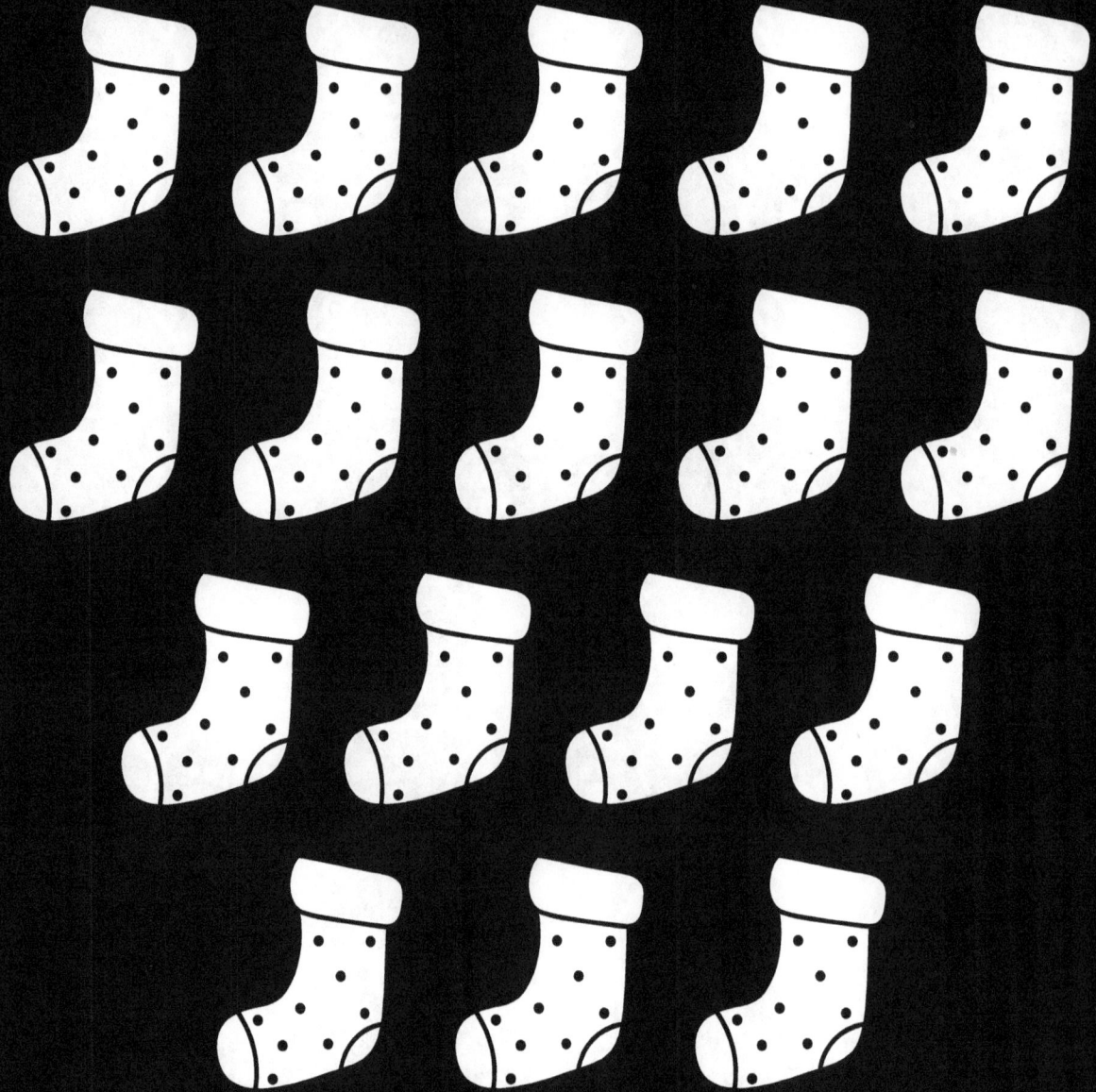

seventeen

17 17 17

I see 18 snowflakes

eighteen

18 18 18

I see 19 Snowmen

nineteen

19 19 19

I see 20 elves

twenty

20 20 20

The number 1

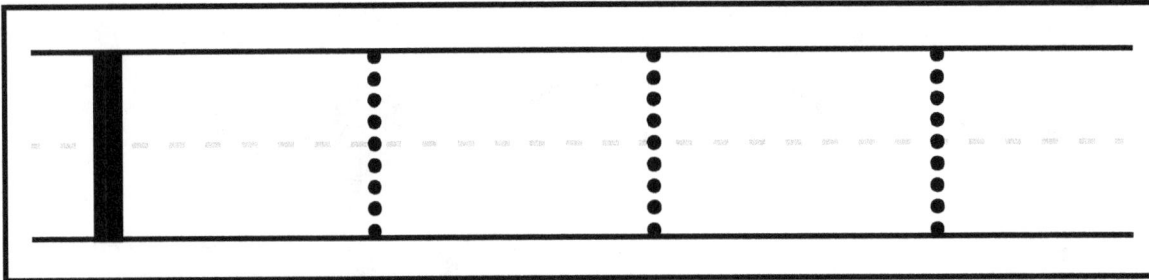

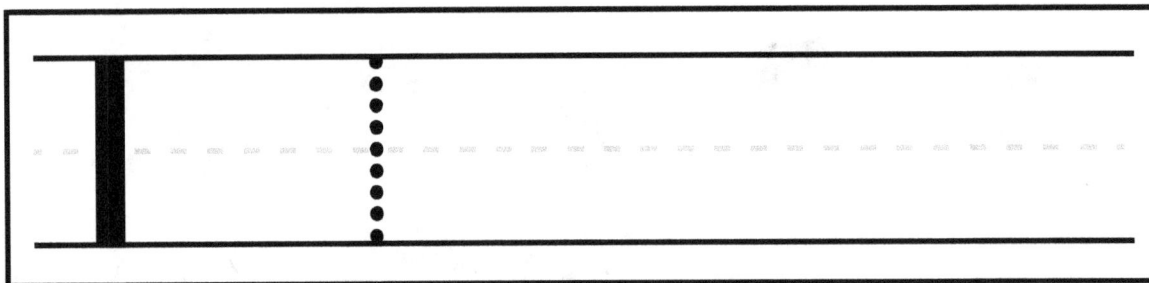

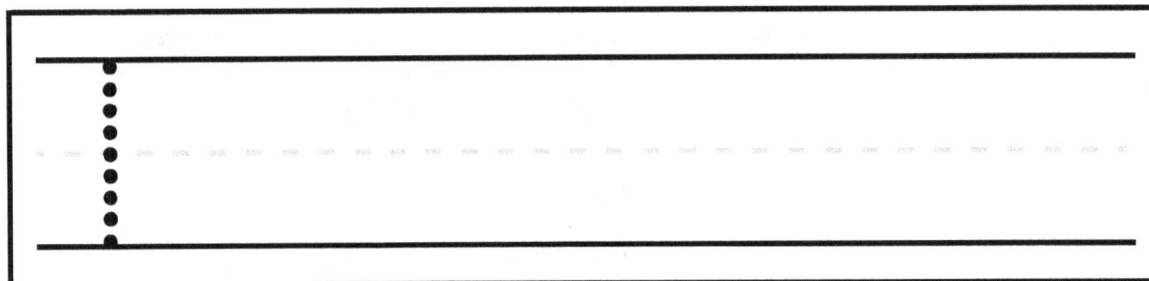

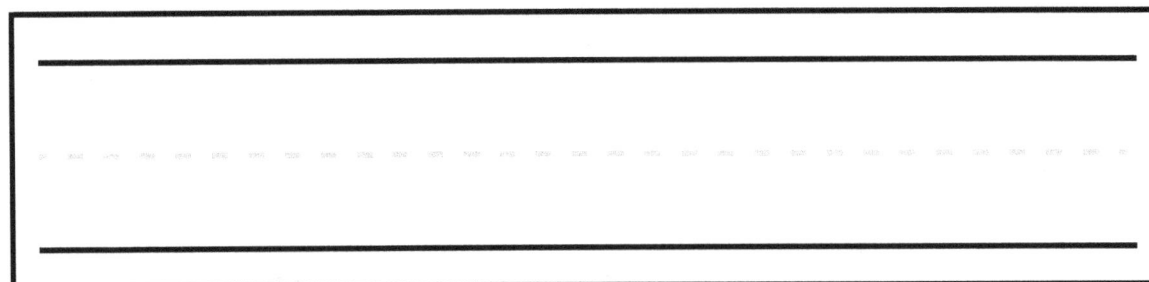

one

 one one

one one

one

The number 2

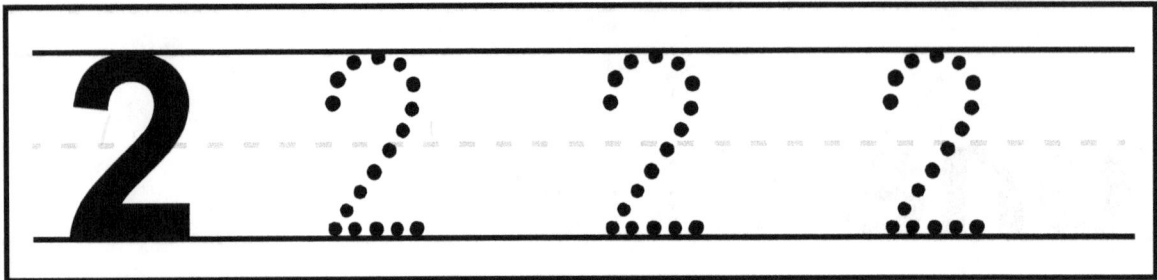

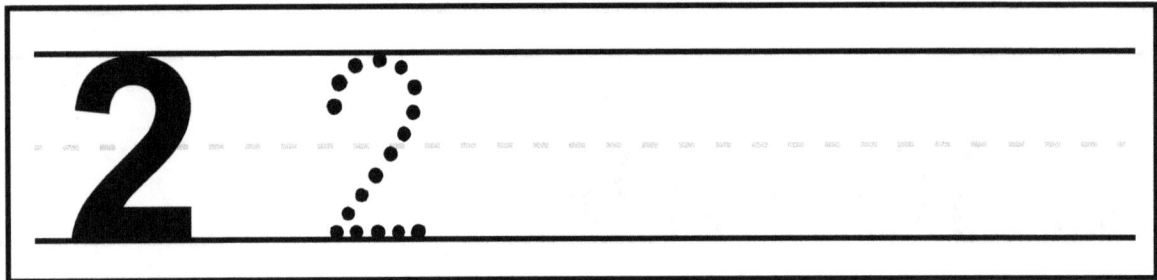

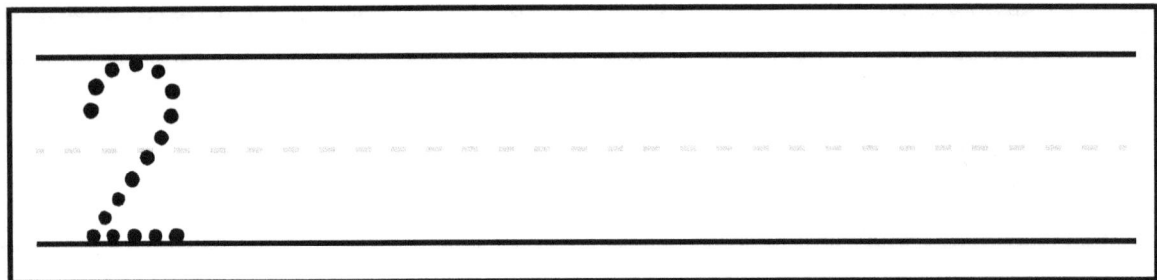

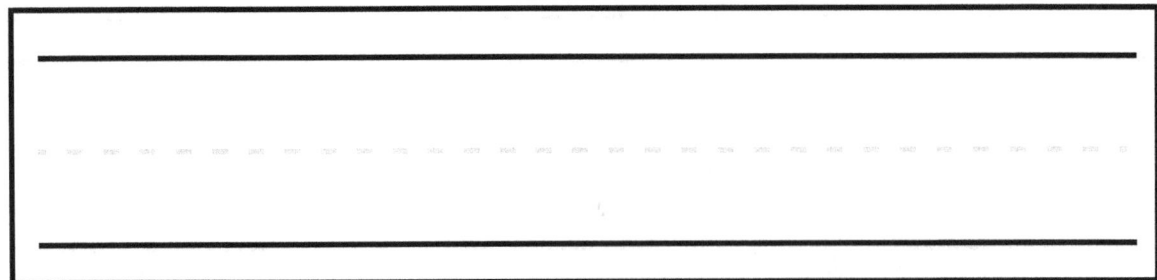

two

two two

two two

two

The number 3

3   3   3   3

3   3

3

three

three three

three three

three

The number 4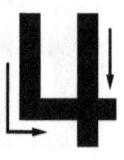

4 4 4 4 4 4 4

4 4

4

four

★ ★ ★ ★

four four

four four

four

The number 5

5 5 5 5

5 5

5

five

★ ★ ★ ★ ★

five five

five five

five

The number 6

6

6

six

★ ★ ★ ★ ★ ★

six six

six six

six

The number 7

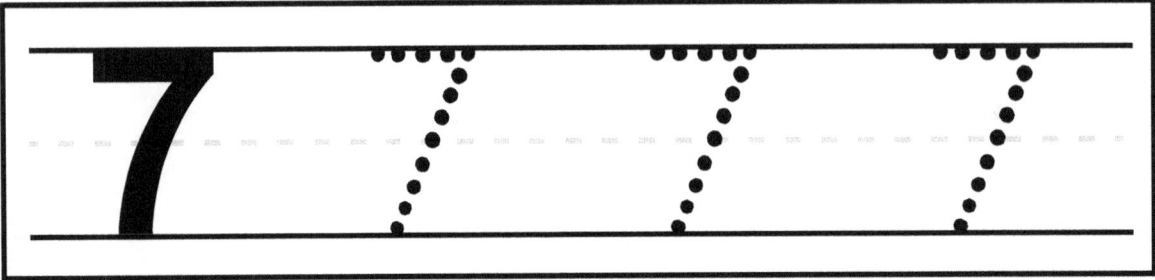

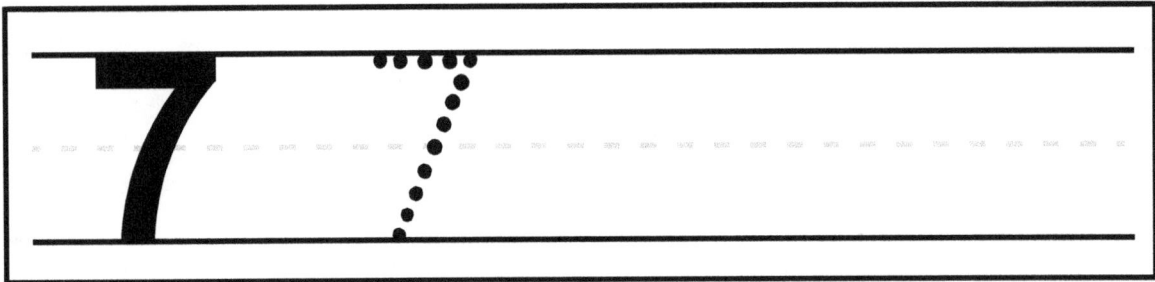

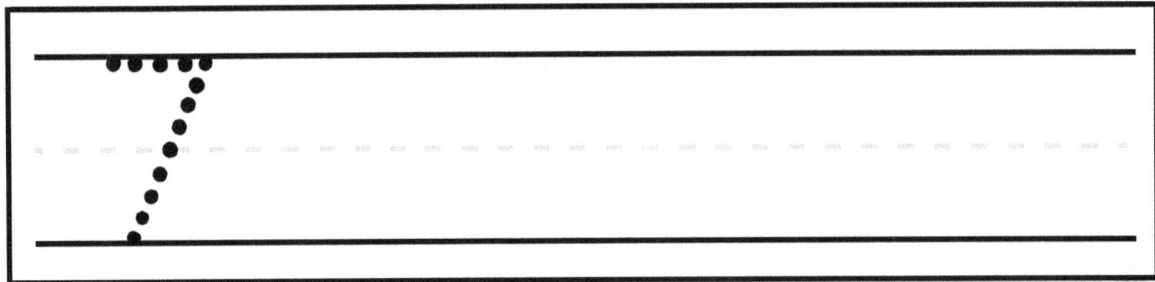

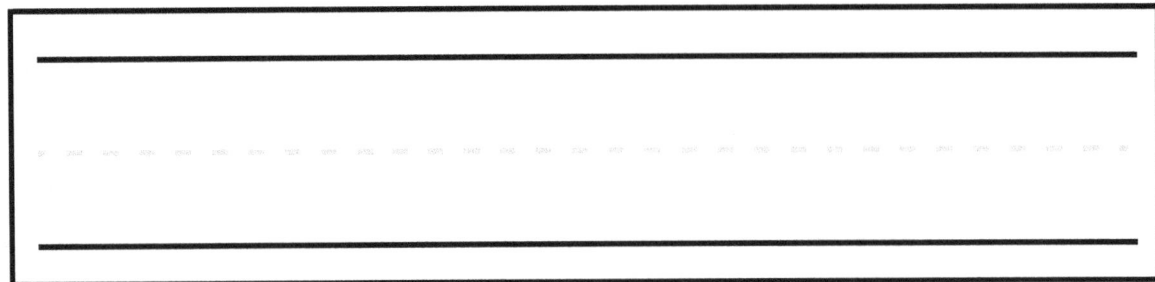

seven

seven seven

seven seven

seven

The number 8

8   8   8   8

8   8

8

eight

eight eight

eight eight

eight

The number 9

9         

9   

nine

nine nine

nine nine

nine

The number 10

10 10 10 10 10

10 10

10

ten

ten ten

ten ten

ten

The number 11

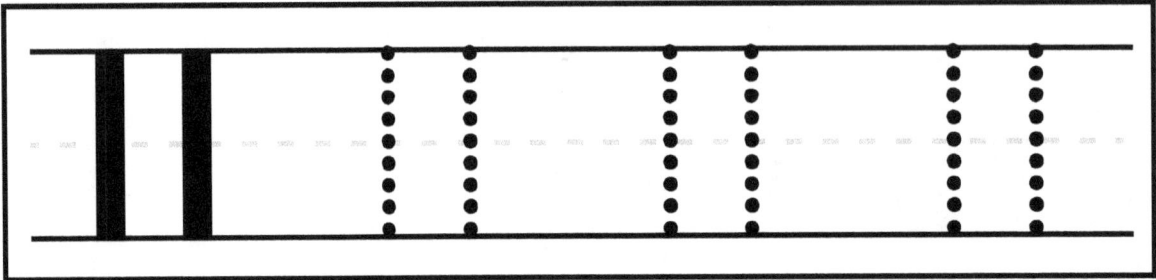

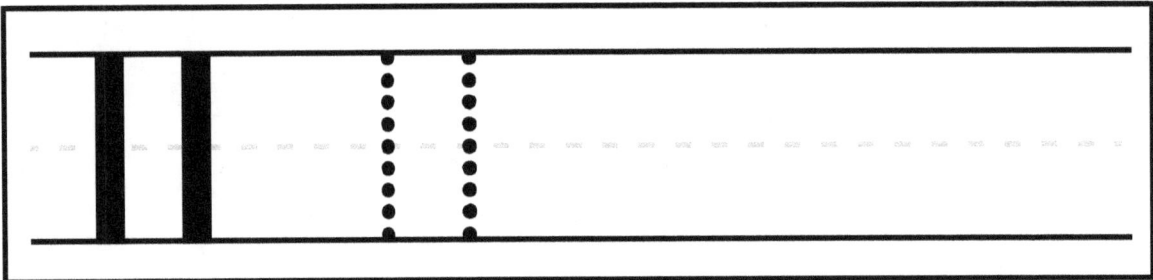

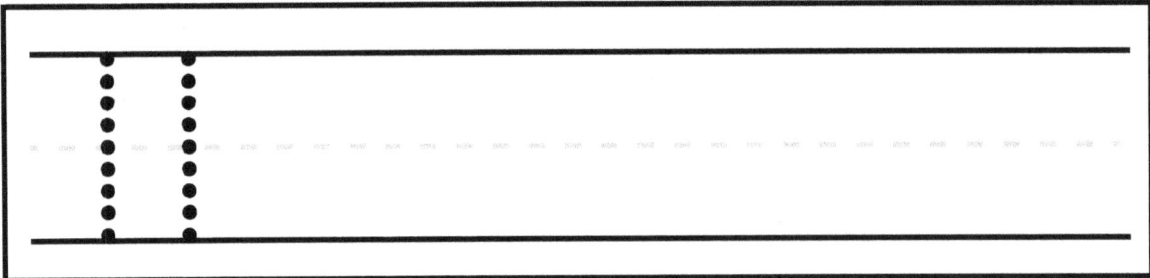

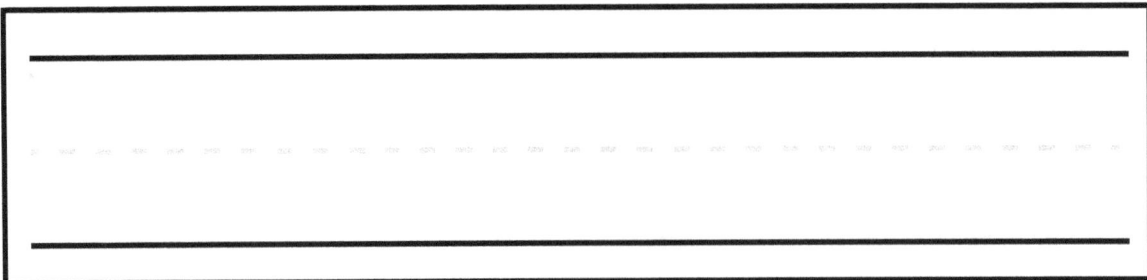

eleven

eleven

eleven

eleven

The number 12

12 12 12 12

12 12

12

twelve

twelve

twelve

twelve

The number 13

13   13   13   13

13   13

13

thirteen

thirteen

thirteen

thirteen

The number 14

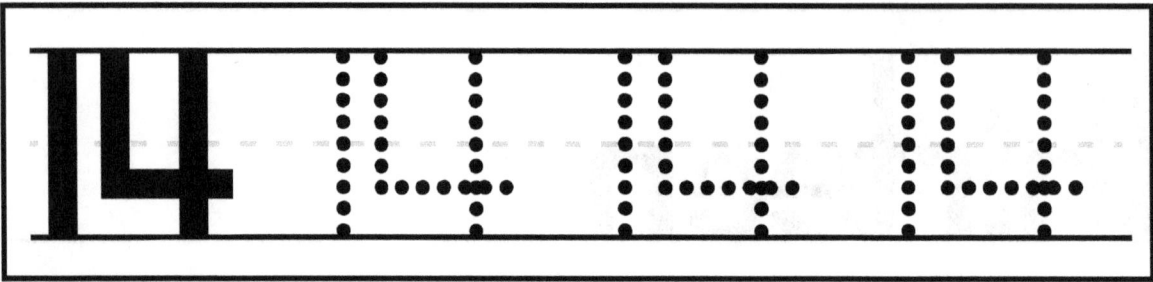

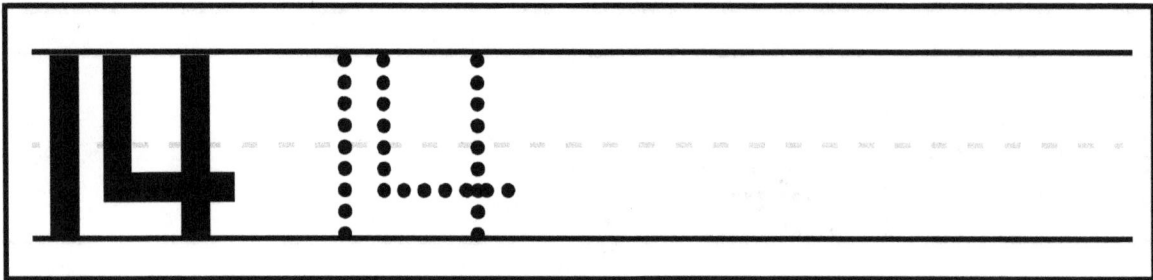

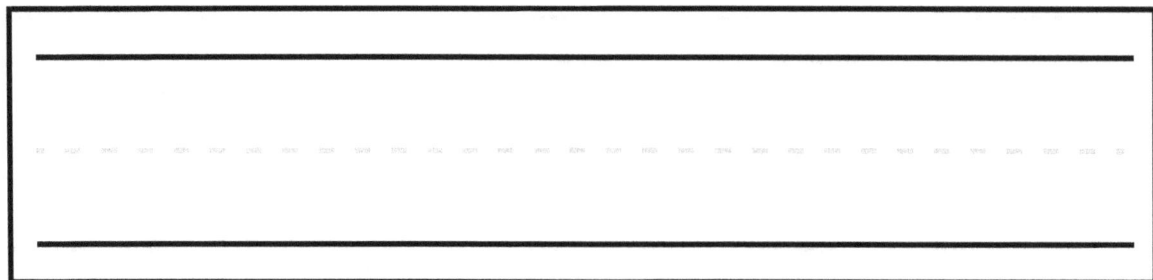

fourteen

fourteen

fourteen

fourteen

The number 15

| 15 | 15 | 15 | 15 |

| 15 | 15 | | |

| 15 | | | |

| | | | |

fifteen

fifteen

fifteen

fifteen

The number 16

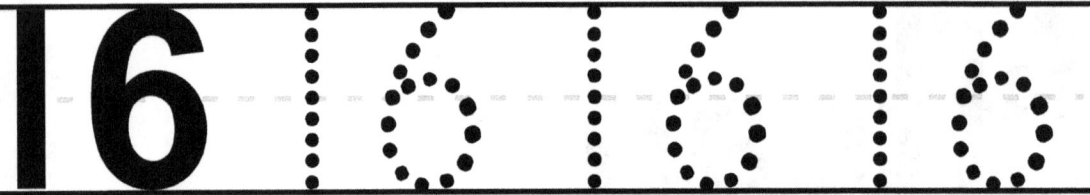

16 16 16 16

16 16

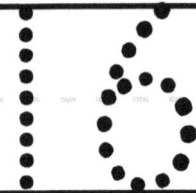

16

sixteen

sixteen

sixteen

sixteen

The number 17

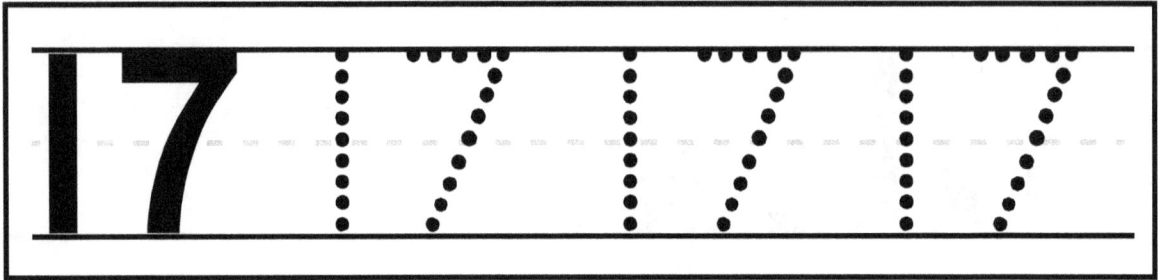

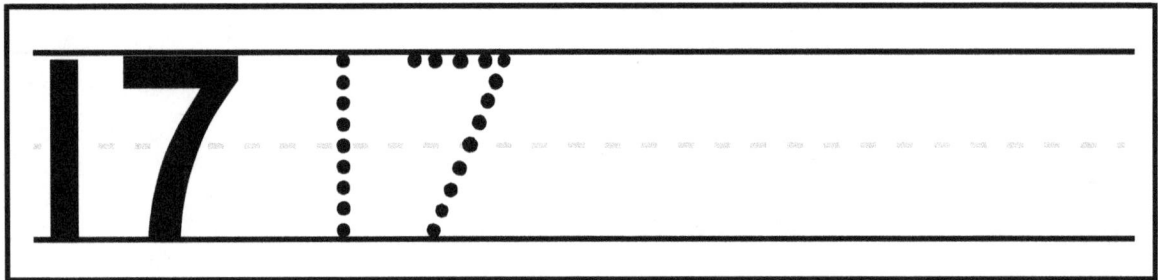

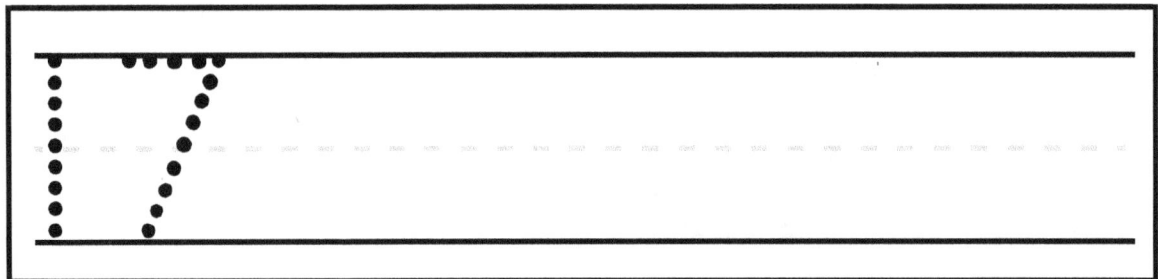

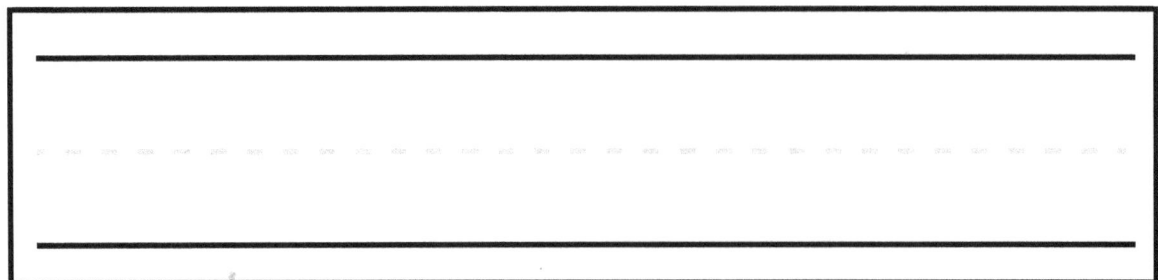

seventeen

seventeen

seventeen

seventeen

The number 18

18 18 18 18

18 18

18

eighteen

eighteen

eighteen

eighteen

The number 19

19   19   19   19

19   19

19

nineteen

nineteen

nineteen

nineteen

The number 20

20 20

20 20

20

twenty

twenty

twenty

twenty

Your Review

What if I told you that just one minute out of your life could bring joy and jubilation to everyone working at a kids art supplies company?
What am I yapping about? I'm talking about leaving this book a review.

I promise you, we take them VERY seriously.

Don't believe me?

Each time right after someone just like you leaves this book a review, a little siren goes off right here in our office. And when it does we all pump our fists with pure happiness.

A disco ball pops out of the ceiling, flashing lights come on…it's party time!
Roger, our marketing guy always and I mean always, starts flossing like a crazy person and keeps it up for awhile. He's pretty good at it. (It's a silly dance he does, not cleaning his teeth)

Sarah, our office manager runs outside and gives everyone up and down the street high fives. She's always out of breath when she comes back but it's worth it!
Our editors work up in the loft and when they hear the review siren, they all jump into the swirly slide and ride down into a giant pit of marshmallows where they roll around and make marshmallow angels. (It's a little weird, but tons of fun)

So reviews are a pretty big deal for us.
It means a lot and helps others just like you who also might enjoy this book, find it too.

YOU'RE THE BEST!
From all of us goofballs at Big Dreams Art Supplies